Margaret

FROM *Ashes*
TO *Glory*

Love in Christ
Pat

FROM *Ashes* TO *Glory*

BY PATRICIA BROWN

XULON PRESS

Xulon Press
2301 Lucien Way #415
Maitland, FL 32751
407.339.4217
www.xulonpress.com

Printed in the United States of America.

ISBN-13: 9781545634455

I dedicate this book to my sister Maureen in heaven. Even through adversity, she showed courage and love.

HIS WORLD

Suppose, in the dawn of creation, in the nothing that was
all around,
God spoke, and the universe listened, obeying His awesome
life-sound,
to form everything as we know it, the stars and the earth
and the seas,
the fish and the sand and the beaches, the rocks and the
flowers, the trees.
Suppose that the last thing created, was formed, as
the symphony
of God's voice spoke love as He breathed sweet life into you
and to me.
Suppose this God made a people, to serve Him and live
in His will;
not because He wanted a family of slaves, but wanted their
lives to be filled.

FROM ASHES TO GLORY

Suppose God sent us a Savior, His very own Son
that He loved,
to die in the place of the whole human race, as He watched,
heart breaking, above.
Suppose He gave us a Scripture, with all that we
needed to grow,
and imagine Him signing it with His own hand, and giving ti
so we would know
how very much He loves us all and watches o'er us every day.
He listens, He speaks, and He cares oh, so much, and He
hears every word when we
pray.
Suppose, just suppose all this happened. Do you think His
holy heart grieves
each time a sinner hears of His works and refuses still
to believe.
If you know He is reaching out to you; if you sense His pow'r
and His might,
don't deny Him, for all that He says is the truth. He will turn
all your darkness to light.
Suppose such a gift was given, and the gift was free and clear,

and suppose it would save you as soon as you took it and
take away all of your fear.
Will you refuse such a treasure? How can you, now
that you know?
You cannot deny that He gave all He had, nor deny how He
loves us all so.
You cannot deny that He gave all He had. It is all in His Word,
and it's true.
He made us, He loves us, and even died for us,
so accept His free gift---it's for you.
The gift is Jesus.

GOD'S GREAT EARTH

Soft as a feather floating on air,

hard as a rock hewn from mountains so rare.

Silent as whispers that waft through the trees,

loud as the roars of thunderous seas.

As lovely as gossamer butterfly wings,

yet sharp when we question the message He brings.

God's Word will e'er stand, whatever we say,

and He says that His Son is life's only Way

for us to be transferred to mansions above,

where He gives, forever, His comfort and love.

So, please don't reject Him nor ignore His plea.

He is the only way we can be free

from all of the wrongs we've committed in vain.

He is the One who can cleanse every stain.

FROM ASHES TO GLORY

Jesus, the Savior is reaching to you,
to wash you and make your life just like brand new.
He died agonizing on Golgotha's hill
to save us and finish His Father's good will.
It's time to decide what your future will be,
endlessly lost or eternally free.

BEAUTY

In the still of the morning, when the skies turn to gold,

as the sun reaches upward in praise;

we magnify Him for His glorious works,

and our hearts worship Him all our days.

In the quiet of night, when the world is asleep

and our weariness claims us to rest,

let us look up and remember the Hope,

and remember how much we are blessed.

SONG

When days seem dark, and clouds have blotted out the light,
and, no matter what we do, it's all an upward climb,
the mountains seem so high sometimes, we feel we'll never
reach the top.
We hang onto our hopes, praying for the sun to shine.
Our troubles feel too heavy for our weakened backs to bear.
Our burdens would be lighter if we had Someone who cared.
Then, suddenly a glimmer breaks into the dusky gloom.
Slowly, gloriously, it begins to fill the room.
It's what we waited for all of the dark days long.
God took our pain and tears and wrote them into song.
God can make a song from all our heartaches and despair;
He changes all the lyrics and clears the gloomy air.
His melody, so sweet that even angels cannot sing.
The song is on our hearts; it's melody, our King.

GOLD

His hands have fashioned all that we see,

His breath has gasped sweet life into me.

His love has given a peace deep inside.

His presence always with me will abide.

My Lord and my Savior gives me everything.

He died for my sins so my crushed heart could sing

a song of rejoicing, a song of new life,

a song for the ending of sorrow and strife.

Jesus has given new life to His fold,

a life that's eternal, more precious than gold.

HOPE

The stable cave is empty where His mother labored through
the night,

bringing forth a Son who would save this wicked world.

The straw has long been swept away, the sheep and cattle gone,

but the promise of that night is here to stay.

The upper room is empty where they supped with the Lord,

as He foretold the pain that was to come;

as He announced that one there would betray Him,

and He would die, God's precious, only Son.

Gethsemane is empty now, where Jesus prayed into the night.

No longer is He bent in agony.

Great drops of blood poured from His pores

as He prayed for sweet release,

and His friends were nearby, lying, fast asleep.

The dusty road is empty now, where He struggled on that day,

stumbling under burdens no one knew.

FROM ASHES TO GLORY

A few felt pity as He valiantly went on,

but most just scorned Him as their hatred grew.

The rugged cross is empty where He hung and bled and died,

taking on the sins of all mankind.

That hate-hewn tree, made by those who tried to silence

His voice, as though to tame the very wind.

The borrowed tomb is empty, too.

O Glorious, wondrous hope.

The tomb where some thought He would always stay.

That rank and airless tomb, that could not keep our Savior

from cheating death and giving us a Way.

The stable, the upper room, the garden, the road, the

cross, the tomb,

all empty of our Savior and our King.

He suffered, died and rose from all the pain and gloom

to save unworthy souls and make our hearts take wing,

and give us all a sweet, new song to sing.

RELIGIOUS?

I used to be religious, as some define the word.

I never missed a Sunday of worshipping the Lord.

I dressed in my best outfit. I sat up front, so proud.

I bowed my head for prayer, and sang the hymns real loud.

I used to be so faithful. I thought that I was good.

I imagined God smiled down on me for doing what I should.

Then, one day someone told me that religion's not enough.

God wants your heart and life and soul, just because of love.

He created all of us to serve Him every day.

He doesn't want a share, a part,

He wants us all the way.

So, I gave Jesus all my heart, according to His Word,

and now I'm not religious.

I just love the Lord.

SUNDAY MORNING

Your morning may have been a mess,
Your tie was missing, your hair askew,
your coffee's cold, you burned the toast
and someone hid your favorite shoes.

The kids are running all around,
and peace seems such a distant hope.
You pray to God for help and strength,
to help you as you try to cope.

You know if you could find your keys,
and get the family out the door
that soon you'd be on down the road,
praising the One this day is for.

You then walk in the open door
where greeters shake your hand and smile,

where hugs are plentiful and warm,
and friends are there to chat a while.
And, as the music starts to play
It penetrates your very soul.
You sing of Jesus and His love,
the songs that never will grow old.
The prayers go up from all the saints,
to Him who hears our every plea.
He smiles on us and blesses us,
and promises eternity.
Jesus died so we could live.
He loved us from the very start.
He knew that we could be His friend,
unworthy, but He saw our hearts.
The pastor tells us of His love
so deep and true, and ever there.
He tells us how to live the life
because he really, truly cares.
Sometimes the words he says are hard,
sometimes we'd like to turn and run.
But, we stay. Where could we go

that offers more than God's dear Son?

He tells the truth, as we must do,

with all our heart and every breath.

He cares enough to ease our doubts,

to save us from a fiery death.

The pastor preaches what he must.

He isn't here to try to please us.

I thank the Lord, for I can tell

that he is so in love with Jesus.

So, let us praise our Lord today,

the mighty Word, God's only Son.

This is all the truth we need;

the only Way, the Holy One.

IF I DIDN'T KNOW BETTER

If I didn't know better, I'd think you were a Christian.

If I didn't know better, I'd think you had the blessing.

You give to all who need your help, you donate money

to the poor.

You go on walks to heal disease. If asked for help, you do

much more.

Your parents are so proud of you. They brag on you to everyone.

You got the highest marks in school, you never leave a

task undone.

You drive the best car in the lot, your house is set high on a hill.

You entertain 'most every week. Your parties give us all a thrill.

Three times a week, you go to church, shaking hands with

every child.

Your hair is neat, your shoes are shined; you eat and drink and

dress in style.

You look like every one's idea of a perfect Christian, and yet, it's hard to profess deep belief in Someone you have never met.

The Bible says your righteousness is nothing more than

filthy rags.

You can't perfect or heal yourself, no matter how your

parents brag.

The Lord looks on your heart, you know. He knows your every

thought and deed.

He loves you, though, no matter what, and He has every-

thing you need.

But works cannot earn you the way to heaven, or to Jesus' side.

So, throw away the pretense please. You are why the Savior died.

He wants your heart, your mind, your soul. He doesn't care what

car you own,

or how much sympathy you give, or how much money

you can loan.

He wants to be the Lord today of all your life, not just a part.

The works you do are emptiness, unless they're done with

Jesus' heart.

Perhaps you can fool all your friends by all you do and

all you say.

But, only God knows how you'll stand when time is come for

judgement day.

Salvation is the only way.

He wants to be the Lord of all your life and not of just a part.

The works you do are emptiness, unless they're done with

Jesus' heart.

A NEW YEAR

The morning fast approaches, the day is coming near.

Another chance, another time to listen, and to hear.

Have you made a resolution, a promise to yourself

to be a better person, improve your body's health?

Have you thought about your future? Will you save

toward a goal?

Do you need a house, a car, a boat or something for your soul?

As you ponder over a new day, think about this too.

What will you do with Jesus? Tell me, what will you do?

He's made it possible for you to live forevermore.

What will you do with Jesus? He's waiting at the door.

Will you go in and stay with Him, the One you should adore?

Will you put your lost hand in His, and call Him Sovereign Lord?

The morning comes so quickly, please make that vow today.

This may be all the chance you have before it goes away.

So, as you plan and ponder, what will your new year bring?

FROM ASHES TO GLORY

What will you do with Jesus?
Close your heart? Or call Him King?

I WAS THERE

I was there when You were born in the manger so very long ago.

I watched as you smiled at Mary, your mother, and she held

you tight,

never wanting to let You go.

I was there when you grew so tall and strong,

I saw how you played and worked day by day.

I saw the way your parents watched you, loving you, as the

years flew away.

I was there as you walked over the land, telling all you met of a

love beyond belief.

I was there as you prayed and wept in the night.

I felt your deep sorrow and your grief.

I remember all the glad times, as people gave their hearts and

lives to you.

I remember the sad times as some taunted you, as deep their

hatred grew.

They didn't understand You, and the love You offered them, so
true and free.
They didn't know that only You were the One to hear their plea.
Sometimes we spurn the very thing we need, though it be given
in Your love.
So, I stood by and watched Your dear heart break
as You wept and prayed to Your Father above.
I was there as Pilate gave his order, and said, "I find no fault
within this Man."
I watched him wash his hands before You, and turn his back as
your torment began.
I was there as you stumbled and fell up the road to Calvary.
I tried to close my eyes that day, to Your pain and agony.
I watched as you hung between two thieves and died.
I wept the tears of all the times that those who loved You cried.
I was there the day the sun shone bright, and the angel said, "He
is no longer here.
He has risen, just the way He said." And You took away
all my fear.
Yes, I was with you all those times, as You are with me now.
You died, and rose again, and still love me somehow.

FROM ASHES TO GLORY

I am but a human, with sins and faults, and strife.

But, you gave all you had that day, for my eternal life.

I was with you then, because You knew my heart,

and You are with me always. We'll never ever part.

Eternity is mine, you love me just the same,

even though, for all Your grief, I am the one to blame.

My live I give to you, o Lord, this is my solemn vow.

You were there when I was born. You knew me fully then.

And you were there the second time,

when I was born again.

OUR DEEPEST
NEEDS

The tiny child softly walked into the village square.

His eyes were sleepy, his hair disheveled, his little feet were bare.

No one noticed his frail, small form as he tried to find a place

where he could stand and listen, and see the Master's face.

Someone finally saw him, tried to send him away.

But, he stood fast and told him, " I'm seeing Jesus today."

The woman trudged on down the lane, her daughter at her heels.

They both were needing something, something very real.

They had heard about the Preacher, who heals the halt and lame.

Though they were well in body, from their soul's deep need

they came.

The Preacher's eyes were kindly. As they listened to His voice,

He spoke with strength and power, asking all to make a choice.

They came to see a preacher, but they found much more that day.

31

FROM ASHES TO GLORY

Some had come to scorn Him, yet many found the Way.

You can hate Him and revile Him. You can say He isn't Lord.

You can keep you heathen ways, still, He won't be ignored.

You may live your life believing you are righteous on you own.

But the Lord Who came to save you, by the sacred life

He gave you,

sees the seeds that you have sown.

His hands are always open, His love his ever here

to take us as we come to Him, no matter how or where.

Don't deny His precious offer, don't forsake the Holy One.

Open your eyes, your heart, your life and accept God's only Son.

ALL I NEED

Give me strength, O Lord, to bear the daily trial,
be my strength as I reach out for Your hand.
Listen as I cry out all my pain and my distress,
lift me from the hardships and the days in sinking sand.
You are all I call for as pain assaults my way.
You are all my help in trouble day by day.
I can feel the joy You give as up to You I climb,
and You reach down and close the gap and give me
hope sublime.
I wasted many years without Your everlasting pow'r,
but now that I have felt it I must have it every hour.
Give me strength, dear Lord, I plead.
You are all I'll ever need.
Your Holy Spirit lives in me
and sets this burdened captive free.
Yes, give me strength, dear Lord, I plead.
You are all I'll ever need.

TRANSFORMATION

I knew a man who drank the cup of bitterness each day.

He hated all men equally and vowed to make them pay.

He'd had a tragic childhood, his parents gave him grief.

He blamed his lot on everyone, yet never found relief.

His bitterness had spread afar, it touched all that he knew.

The more he spoke of all his trials, the more his hatred grew.

Then, one day someone came to him, a smile on his face.

Without a fear he told this man of God's amazing grace.

He told a tale of love so sweet, it reaches out to all.

It frees us from our mortal sin and tears down every wall.

He told this bitter, tortured man that Jesus died one day

to show a love, a love that none on earth could take away.

It wasn't easy reaching one whose life was wracked with pain.

When one has lived in hatred's heat, it's hard to feel the rain.

But, love reached down and touched his soul and joy filled up

his heart.

FROM ASHES TO GLORY

He felt a peace he'd never felt. God gave a brand new start.

His past was not a pretty one, but Jesus will forgive.

He'll cleanse us and He'll free us and show us how to live.

Each person has a deep heart need, to know that he is loved.

And how can any person love as much as God above?

When Jesus came to die for us, He did it willingly,

because He knew He is the Way to set our spirits free.

A man, a woman and a child; love's created ones,

need Jesus Christ the Savior, God's precious, only Son.

So, if your past is hard to take, if today is trying, too,

take a moment, stop, and take the gift He has given you.

He's waiting always patiently, He's standing at the door.

He wants to heal, He wants to help,

and no one loves you more… than Jesus.

THE WAY

Some days we feel deserted, we look around and see
destruction, crime and mayhem by evil pow'rs that be.
This world we now reside in is not the one we knew
when we were young and innocent, believing as we grew,
that all our cares and troubles were only for a while.
That we would all come through them, and later we could smile.
Yet, God has not forgotten. His love remains the same.
He grieves because the sin we do is causing all our pain.
He stands forever ready to cleanse us and forgive.
He knows our hearts are broken each day we strive to live.
We were created to praise His Name,
not for our glory, nor for any fame.
We cannot make a difference without our Savior's aid.
This striving in our own strength negates the price He paid.
No matter what else happens, if we are bound or free,
Jesus is the answer, the Way for you and me.

DEPRESSION

Depression comes down like a cloud on your heart,
it hangs like the gloom of despair,
and nothing can move it, you feel, as you fall
to your knees and utter a prayer.
Your faith is small as you speak to the Lord,
you hope He can hear you at all.
You wait for His answer in the darkness around,
doubting He heard your faint call.
Then, through the deep mist shines a beacon of light,
your heart feels like air on a wing.
The peace settles in and you breathe in relief,
for you are in touch with the King.
Your life may be empty of joy or of peace,
your heart may just dread every day,
but, no matter how far down the well of despair,
we'll be healed if we take time to pray.

FROM ASHES TO GLORY

Talk to Him now in your deepest, dark pain,

tell Him your sorrows, your loss.

There's nothing that Jesus won't help you get through.

Just take all your pain to the cross.

The sunshine will come in the sweetness of peace,

He'll surround you with joy and with love.

With our Savior around we have nothing to fear,

all help that we need is above.

Talk to Him now in your deepest dark pain,

tell Him your sorrows, your loss.

There's nothing that Jesus won't help you get through;

Just take all your pain to the cross.

HEALING JOY

When the sky falls down around you, and the ground is
sinking sand;
when your last best friend has hurt you, and your life sifts
through your hands,
when the little things that plague you seem much to big to stand,
and the pressures and the stresses are an ever-tightening band;
take a moment to remember Who's been right here through it all.
He's waiting and He's wondering why He's the last One you call.
If you'd only cry out to Him, and trust Him all along,
then you'd realize how much God wants to make your
life a song.
His music may be silent when its peace you're yearning for.
Or he can write a symphony when your heart cries out for more.
God loves you every moment. His wish is that His tune
could play its chords from heaven's door to reach your own
heart's room.

If you would only let Him, He would turn the tears and pain
of life's hard road to glorious song and give you joy again.
Just cling to Him and sing with Him that beautiful refrain;
the song that heals, the song that fills your life with love's
sweet rain.

HEAVEN

Heaven....I've always wanted to go there,

plan to as a matter of fact.

What are your plans for eternity?

Are you living pipe dreams of reincarnation?

Are you deluding yourself that you are Alright because

you are good,

or never smoked, or never swear, yell at your kids or speed

in traffic?

Are you aiming for a higher plane? Or do you want the Truth?

Here it is....

God made you. He made me. He reigns over the earth, the sun,

the sky, the lakes,

the mountains, and He made the Rules.

And His number one rule is......

you cannot come to Him except through His Son.

Son, you ask? God has a Son? Yes, His name is Jesus, and He
loves you,
and He loves me, and He created heaven so we could
be His eternally.
So, plan to go there, but plan your route by way of Calvary, and
through the
fountain of blood. You will make it. I will see you there.

DEFINITIONS

TRAVELING

Going on a journey, if you have the means.

It you know the direction. Perhaps you get waylaid,

maybe you get lost… but you always had the Map.

It is called the Word of God.

TRAVAILING

Agonizing. Worrying over what we think are large prob-

lems.. caring,

but not understanding.. hurting, but not forever.

The answer.. you know it.

It's the Word.

TURNING

You were going in circles…

you still do at times.. no direction..

if you turn.. you should turn right.

That is where you will find it.

The Word.

TAKING

No more traveling in vain…

No more travailing in pain…

No more turning with nothing to gain… only

going God's Way… He is the Word, and He

knows the true Meaning. Jesus the Lord, the real Word.

THE WALL

The wall is there, and we have built it
solid, strong, and, stone by stone,
it closes out the world around us,
leaving us so all alone.
We want no feelings penetrating,
this wall that will let no one near;
no good, no bad, no joy, no sad,
and, yet, we still have all our fear.
What can't get in is help we need,
and all that stays is hurt and pain.
They came along, they're ours alone,
they travelled on our pity train.
We need to look around ourselves,
to see and feel and touch and hear,
to sense the Presence of the One
Who always wants to stay so near.

FROM ASHES TO GLORY

Whatever pain and hurts we feel,

He's felt them deeper than we know;

the agonies of life's sore trials,

every sorrow, every woe.

He walked the road before we came,

to be assured that we could, too.

He suffered all and did not fail

to make a way for me and you.

So, if you live behind a wall

and cannot rid yourself of grief,

remember that our Lord is there

to give us all His sweet relief.

His hand is out, his arms are warm,

His Word is true forevermore.

His promises were made for us.

Where we build walls, He carved a Door.